PUFFIN BOOKS

HELLO, 21ST CENTURY

Also in conjunction with Blue Peter

ANIMALS MATTER

Blue Peter

Hello, 21st Century

Illustrated by Tony Ross

PUFFIN BOOKS

PUFFIN BOOKS

Published by the Penguin Group
Penguin Books Ltd, 27 Wrights Lane, London W8 5TZ, England
Penguin Books USA Inc., 375 Hudson Street, New York, New York 10014, USA
Penguin Books Australia Ltd, Ringwood, Victoria, Australia
Penguin Books Canada Ltd, 10 Alcorn Avenue, Toronto, Ontario, Canada M4V 3B2
Penguin Books (NZ) Ltd, 182–190 Wairau Road, Auckland 10, New Zealand

Penguin Books Ltd, Registered Offices: Harmondsworth, Middlesex, England

First published 1993
10 9 8 7 6 5 4 3 2 1

Typeset by Datix International Limited, Bungay, Suffolk
Filmset in 13/15 pt Monophoto Plantin
Printed in England by Clays Ltd, St Ives plc

CONTENTS

FOREWORD

What will the future bring? It's the big
question. *Blue Peter* viewers who took part in
our 'Hello 21st Century' competition came up
with some fascinating answers. As we hurtle
towards the twenty-first century, with changes
taking place at an ever-increasing pace, the
future seems like a murky fog to adults – to
the children who took part in our competition,
it's crystal-clear!

25,201 people sent their ideas, forecasting a
world with every kind of possibility – where
there's enough to eat, no diseases and no wars.
Less optimistic are the ideas which see
continuing damage to the environment. These
contributions carry the message 'act now to
stop this happening'.

Buying this book does more than star-gaze into the future. It will help children right now, as the proceeds all go to Readathon, the sponsored reading event, and then on to the Malcolm Sargent Cancer Fund for Children and The Roald Dahl Foundation.

Finally, a forecast of my own. I hope *Blue Peter* and Puffin will still be joining forces to bring children the very best in the twenty-first Century!

Lewis Bronze
Editor, *Blue Peter*

1

HELLO, 21ST CENTURY

Hello, 21st Century

All cars are computerized
so to go your own way,
you tap in some numbers
then you're off for the day.

At school there're no teachers
all you have is a video,
you tap in some numbers
for what you need to know.

The houses are homely
all made from metal,
you tap in some numbers
then on goes the kettle.

The shops are all glass
with plenty on the shelf,
you tap in some numbers
then just help yourself.

All our pets are robots
cuddly they are not,
you tap in some numbers
the response is fantastic!

2ND PRIZE WINNER – 8s, 9s, 10s

CLAIRE MARSDEN   AGE 9   HULL

Living in the Twenty-first Century

Solar panels and satellite TV,
How old-fashioned they are to me.
Our home is heated direct from Mars,
The TV station is amongst the stars.

Our nuclear cooker produces our meals,
Nutritious and healthy, how good we feel.
It's computer for this, touch-button for that,
Even the robots have time for a chat.

The World is all fed, we've planted more
    trees,
The ozone layer is all in one piece.
No plastics or rubbish, we recycle them all,
The days gone by are hard to recall.

Tutorials are over, technology is all done,
Graduation is over, the prizes all won.
The space buggy's ready, we'll be away soon,
For our vacation this year, we're off to the
moon.

STRUAN RUSSON   AGED 10   ALBRIGHTON WOLVERHAMPTON

In the Year 2000

In the year 2000
I bet it will be fun,
Might have lots of robots,
Who make the adults RUN.

In the year 2000
The cars will all be green,
And the biggest greenest car
Will be driven by the QUEEN.

In the year 2000
I hope there'll be *no* war,
I also hope that people,
Will be poor no MORE.

ANNA LOUISE HUTT   AGE 7   FARNHAM, SURREY

Dear Diary

The new teacher is a real WEIRDO.
Yesterday, he came in and told us we were
going on a trip.

'Not the library again!' I said. (New
teachers always take us there.)

'No, not the library,' he said. He pulled a
little black box out of his pocket. 'What do
you think this is?'

Everyone peered at the box, but I saw what
it was straight away. 'It's a Walkman.'

'No, it's not.' (He sounded quite serious.)
'It's a time-machine. We're going into the
future.'

Honestly! What did he think we were? The
others kids gaped, but I stared out of the
window, to show him what I thought of his
stupid games.

Then he began to hand out brown paper
bags.

'Your eyes will need covering. Put one of
these on your head.'

Paper bags? Did he think we were idiots? I
wasn't going to put mine on, but he gave me
such a glare that I didn't dare not to.

'Now, let's all think about what we might be
going to see,' he said. 'What will the future be
like?'

All the boys started calling out ridiculous
things.

'Robots everywhere, sir!'

'Hyper-speed cars!'

'Brain transplants!'

I lifted up the edge of my paper bag. 'The future won't be like that at all.' (Don't they know anything?) 'The rain forests will be chopped down, and the ice-caps will melt because of global warming. Everything will have to be recycled, and all the animals will be extinct –'

I could have gone on, but *he* wouldn't let me.

'That's enough. I'm going to activate the time-machine.'

They actually believed him! Can you imagine it? Some of them even started screaming through their paper bags.

'No, sir! We don't want to go! It'll be horrible!'

He started his countdown. 'Five, four, three –'

'PLEASE, sir!'

'– two, one –'

'Don't switch on!'

'ZERO!! We're on our way!'

I pulled off my paper bag and (surprise, surprise!) everything was exactly the same. No global warming, and no flooding in the playground. Just Alice Mitchell, sneaking in late as usual.

'You don't need to worry,' I said. 'It's only a game.'

They all started pulling off their bags, and *he* gave me a very funny look.

'A game?'

'People can't get into the future,' I said.

He raised his eyebrows. 'But we're travelling into the future at this very moment. At 3600 seconds per hour.'

For a second, I felt really odd. But I couldn't let him beat me. I sniffed, and stared out of the window for the rest of the lesson.

When I came to do the homework I said just what I thought. *The future is in the future.* I wrote. *People can't get there.*

Then I went into the garden, to help my dad chop down the oak tree.

GILLIAN CROSS

The Sale of the Century

I was bored with the Twenties,
And I did have some money,
So I went to the shops,
To buy a new century.

They were fresh out at Woollies,
And Argos had none.
I even tried Harrods,
To find a nice one.

The new-age departments,
In all of the stores,
Had loads of new centuries,
On each of the floors.

Some centuries were peaceful,
But nothing much happened,
And I needed excitement,
Or I'd go round the bend.

A few were quite good,
But others were not,
They had wars and pollution,
And things got too hot.

Then I found my favourite,
(All peace and harmony),
In the catalogue at Index,
But it cost too much money.

In the end I settled,
For a good and bad mixture,
It was labelled twenty-first,
And I got a good fixture.

And the good thing about it,
Was all that it cost,
Was good human nature,
Which we seem to have lost.

TANYA PEMBERTON   AGE 15   THORNTON HEATH, SURREY

Dear Century,

I'm returning the package of all out war that was on offer in your catalogue. I don't need it, dear Century, because, dear Century, it hurts, it costs too much and anyway, it doesn't work.
                    Michael Rosen

First broadcast on Blue Peter *in October 1992 and reproduced by kind permission of the author.*

Letter to the Manager of the 21st Century

World Headquarters
Great North Road
Morpeth
Northumberland

Ms Nkoto
Laascaanood
Somalia
Africa

Dear Ms Nkoto,

As outgoing members of the board of directors of the 20th century, we are delighted to offer you the position of Manager of the 21st century.

We were particularly impressed by your attitude to the following problems, and hope you will address them quickly.

1. World food shortage. Your plan to ration food supplies worldwide is interesting. The idea that people in the developed world should eat less (and so reduce obesity, diabetes, heart disease, etc.) so that people in the less developed countries have more is not new, but we feel that you propose an imaginative solution.

2. World Resources. The need to conserve resources has been obvious in the 20th century. Your plan to provide the world's energy entirely from sun, wind, water and the earth's heat is promising. We hope your developments (including the ban on private transport) are in place before the current supplies run out.

3. Conflict. Unfortunately, we cannot see an easy answer to these problems. However, your determination to reach a solution is commendable. We feel that sharing the world's wealth should reduce greed. Your commitment to power-sharing between races, creeds, religions, sexes, ages, etc. is admirable.

Your starting date is 00.00 hours on 1 January 2000. The newly elected board of directors will be pleased to welcome you.
   We wish you well.

Yours sincerely
R. Fraser
Secretary

RACHEL FRASER   AGE 13   MORPETH, NORTHUMBERLAND

Saying Hello to the Twenty-first Century!

H is for **H**appiness, that's what we need.
E is for **E**xercise planting seeds.
L is for **L**aughter, happy faces too.
L is for **L**eaves in the morning dew.
O is for **O**ak trees, big and strong.

T is for **T**oads, hopping along.
W is for **W**ind, whistling a song.
E is for **E**agle, flying in the sky.
N is for **N**ature, a cool breeze drifting by.
T is for **T**iger, standing proud.
Y is for **Y**oung people, singing aloud.

F is for **F**ish, swimming in the sea.
I is for **I**vory, please let it be.
R is for **R**ainbow, bright in the sky.
S is for **S**tars, shooting so high.
T is for **T**omorrow, it's another day.

C is for **C**hildren, show them the way.
E is for **E**nvironment, it needs our care.
N is for **N**ectar, for the bees to share.
T is for **T**urtles, there to protect.
U is for **U**niverse, we must not neglect.
R is for **R**abbits, running wild and free.
Y is for **Y**ou and me, in peace and harmony!

LEILA BADAOUI   AGE 9   WEST BRIDGFORD, NOTTINGHAM

Futuristic Wordsearch

Can you find these fifteen words either
forwards, backwards, up, down or diagonally
in the square below?

ROBOT	HOLOGRAM
SPACECAR	LASER
MACHINE	SONICBALL
COMPUTER	ROCKET
SCIENCE	MOON
SPACE CITY	MODERN
ASTRONAUT	FUTURE
TECHNOLOGY	

T	A	R	O	B	E	E	S	C	I	E	N	C	E	S
U	E	O	B	U	Z	M	X	O	Y	P	Z	C	N	D
A	T	C	N	R	E	D	O	M	H	G	Y	E	I	I
N	D	K	H	A	L	J	F	P	V	W	L	J	H	M
O	U	E	O	N	U	Y	S	U	F	L	A	X	C	O
R	R	T	L	R	O	B	O	T	T	D	S	N	A	O
T	A	F	O	C	Q	L	T	E	Q	U	E	B	M	N
S	X	H	G	I	T	G	O	R	K	W	R	P	L	V
A	W	N	R	F	K	C	R	G	N	I	O	E	H	Z
E	S	P	A	C	E	C	I	T	Y	V	F	R	M	M
G	C	G	M	L	L	A	B	C	I	N	O	S	K	A
O	Q	S	D	B	P	R	A	C	E	C	A	P	S	J

SARAH PEARSE   AGE 10   GERMANY

2

A FUTURE FOR ALL THE WORLD

A Saying

We look forward to the 21st century when we children will make history.

We shall be the doctors who will cure the common cold.

We shall be the animal lovers who will save the rare breeds.

We shall be the scientists who will invent ways to clean up the world.

We shall be the politicians who make peace in the world and help the poor.

We shall also have the fun of driving flying cars and having holidays on the moon.

NICOLA STORRING   AGE 7   WANSTEAD, LONDON

HANNAH SHARPE   AGE 15   RYDE, ISLE OF WIGHT

Red, Yellow or Green?

We hold the future key now, we are the hope of the world now. Which door should we take, which choice should we make? The key will fit all three locks.

Should we go through the RED door into

darkness and despair, to a lifeless black hole where humans thrive, where war has torn the world apart, where people are dying of food poisoning in their millions.

Or should we go through the YELLOW door into a world of mixed feelings, some people are rich, some are poor, some are evil and some are good, some are happy, some are sad, and pollution is rising to a dangerous level. In short the world is on the brink of disaster.

Or should we take the GREEN door into a world of peace, where animals and people can thrive side by side, and the only things that have become extinct are war and pollution.

IAN MACDONALD   AGE 10   OXFORD

My Wishes for the 21st Century

Health and happiness for everyone.
Act quickly to save the environment.
Peace for everyone – no more wars.
Pollution will disappear.
Innocent animals will not be killed.
Northern Ireland will become peaceful
Earth will be a beautiful place to live.
Starvation will come to an end . . .
So that there will be something left for the
    young.

SCOTT MARLEY   AGE 7   WIDNES, CHESHIRE

Hello! Twenty-first Century

Hello, twenty-first century,
    It's great to be here at last.
I'm looking forward to a new kind of life,
    But I'll never forget the past.

Maybe I'll travel in a spaceship,
    To visit Jupiter, Venus or Mars.
Or even go much further,
    And discover more new stars.

But no matter what is promised,
    In my new life here with you,
I won't forget the struggles,
    This earth has been put through.

Toxic waste, pollution, destruction,
    Wars, famine, and many deaths.
Through man's own self-domination,
    He almost caused your final breath.

But he realized in time,
    What to do to put it right.
And thanks to all the nations
    Coming together, seeing the light!

We've arrived here safely to meet you,
    With one aim in all our sights,
To live in peace and harmony,
    And this time get it right.

And as each day and year goes by,
    Appreciate the world we have,
And strive to keep it growing
    And NEVER LET IT DIE.

GILES HIBBERD   AGE 13   NEWPORT, GWENT

Bon Appetit!

The *Monseigneur* stood on the steps of the church of *Sainte Marie de Piana*, having just celebrated the last two hundred years of the building's history. Wearing his gold bishop's mitre, and with a modern crook blazing in the sun, *Monseigneur* Casanova blessed one and blessed all. The Corsican village was out in its Sunday clothes, the older men quiet in their jackets, the women in their floral frocks kissing the holy hand, the children being led forward to have a blessing put gently upon their heads. The mayor, tall and dignified in his French sash of red, white and blue, waited patiently while the timid and the reluctant were brought forward to be smiled upon by the *Monseigneur*.

Later in the day, the cross from the altar and an effigy of the Madonna would be carried through the village, between high walls, over cobbles, through the dust, with the children holding hands in front, the women singing *Ave Maria* next, and the men talking quietly at the rear, a tradition centuries older than the 1792 church. But now, at half-past-twelve, on these same church steps that had heard proclamations of war and of peace, and of every important event in people's lives, at the end of the morning's proceedings, when there was no one left to be blessed, the *Monseigneur* opened wide his arms for a final pronouncement. The crowd went quiet, the mayor turned to give his full attention, patting his jacket pockets in a small nervous gesture. The nearer children stopped their games. '*Bon appetit!*' the *Monseigneur* said, smiling, nodding, and with a last wave he returned into the church to change for lunch. *Bon appetit!* And something else he had added, hardly heard because it was under his breath. *Bon appetit!* The traditional French benediction: because in their turn events eventually come round to food. And so Piana went to its lunch: the *Monseigneur* to the best hotel, tourists to the restaurants, the villagers to their shaded Sunday tables. *Bon appetit!*

This was 1992. And what of this day a hundred years on, when the tricentenary of the church is being celebrated, when even the children leading the procession today will be lying silent in the cemetery facing the sea? Will they, who today were closest to the *Monseigneur*, have heard the message in the words he muttered after *Bon appetit!*?

A tout le monde?

And will they, in their lifetime, have done anything to make his wish come true?

BERNARD ASHLEY

One Meal a Day Cake

4 micro eggs
2 pts of milk
1 bar of chocolate
1 bag of pasta
2 loaves of bread
90 vitamin pills
veg mix
fruit
2 cheese slices

Put all the ingredients in a bowl and mix with
a whizz whisk. Pour into a tin and bake for
1 minute in the super-speedy micro cooker.
Serve to whole family with pleasure and enjoy
the rest of the day.

LAUREN SANDERCOME   AGE 6   ENFIELD, MIDDLESEX

What I Hope

The next century draws near;
hopeful and reticent we wait for it – shadowed
   by pangs of fear.
We are ambiguous, as to what to expect.
But nevertheless we contemplate and reflect.

Lost in a world of hopes and dreams.
Even the improbable is left to gleam.
Reality is put aside;
and our dreams are let loose – on a vivacious
   ride.

It's like being given a ticket, to the unknown.
But we accept that ticket, our boldness not
    shown.
Maybe by the next century, there will be a
    better way of life.
Immortal happiness in our world; not
    continuous strife.

There would be no more war.
Of that we can be sure.
Our differences would be solved in an
    amicable way.
Everyone, no matter how small, shall have
    their say.
And the sun shall shine merrily every day.

The environment shall remain intact.
And that my fellow, you can consider a
    possible fact.

All these tribulations will not count.
And all the troubles in the world will work
    themselves out.
There will be no killing or bloodshed.
And every hungry soul in the world will be
    fed.

My hope for the next century is small and
    simple:
for all the suffering in the world to decease.
And for us, as a whole, to achieve eternal
    peace.

'What a dreamer,' I hear you cry.
'Maybe I am,' I reply with a heavy sigh.
'But all I want is peace of mind.
And all everyone wants is peace – for all
    mankind.'

SHAZIA PARVEEN   AGE 14   SMALL HEATH, BIRMINGHAM

Recipe For The Year 2000
Blend together Peace and
Harmony. Add a little
Understanding. Then, gradually
fold in Tender Loving Care,
Health and Happiness. Mix
all the remaining best
ingredients of Life together
to make a better World to live in.

CHRISTOPHER STONE   AGE 8   STOKE-ON-TRENT, STAFFS

3

REMARKABLE ROBOTS

Me and Zap

I have a friend. His name is Zap. He is silver
and white. He is a robot. They made him out
of Dad's old car. He likes me. He likes playing
catch and football. When I tickle him, it
makes him laugh. Sometimes he walks to
school with me. I tell him secrets; he's good
at keeping them. Yesterday I told him there
would be no more fighting. I hope there
won't. He smiled at me, he knows everything.
I feel safe.

1ST PRIZEWINNER – 7s and under

DERWIN GREGORY   AGE 6   CHELMSFORD, ESSEX

Roger the Robot That Helps Disabled People

1. Telephone receiver
2. Coffee and tea maker
3. Braille TV
4. Radio
5. Can-opener for cat and dog food

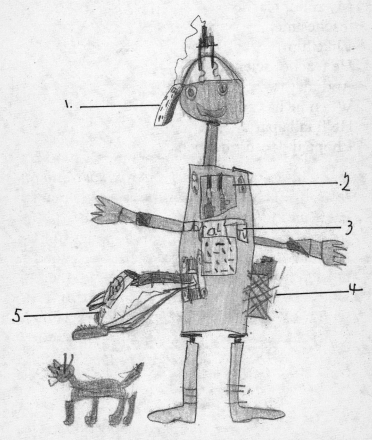

SAM BLAYER   AGE 6   STAINES, MIDDLESEX

Robot Teacher

My robot teacher
teaches me.
I don't like him,
He doesn't teach PE.
When I fall over
And hurt myself,
He doesn't cuddle me.

My robot teacher
teaches me.
I like him,
He teaches science
And maths.
When he has grown old,
He'll fall apart.
I hope it doesn't happen.

NEIL COLLINS   AGE 6   DUSTON, NORTHAMPTON

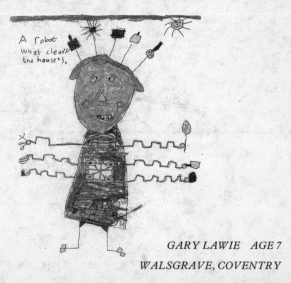

A robot
what cleans
the houses.

GARY LAWIE   AGE 7
WALSGRAVE, COVENTRY

A Future *Blue Peter* Presenter

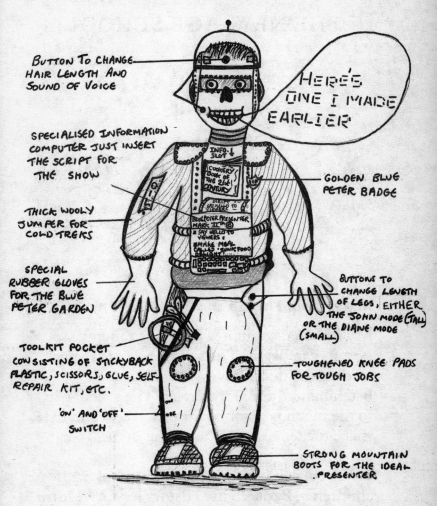

RICHARD CARPENTER   AGE 15   WATFORD, HERTS

4

THE NEW-AGE SCHOOL

My School Day in the 21st Century

My personal computer is plugged in, my lessons can begin. The school robots are busy loading the microwaves for lunch, and listening to the children read. The school trip to the moon is planned for next week, and the space rocket is already standing in the playground.

My French lesson is by satellite-link with children in Paris. In my History lesson we learn about the Yugoslavian war of 1992. What is a war? There aren't any in the 21st century. When school finishes, I go home in my electric car.

LUCY EVANS   AGE 6   HAZLEMERE, BUCKS

School's Cool

School isn't brilliant.
School isn't fab.
School is just boring.
School's just a drag.
But that will all change
For the very first time.
In the 21st century
School will be fine.
You won't have to write
Till your arm starts to ache.
Just press a few keys
That's all it will take.
Our teacher will be
A robot instead.
One without eyes in
Both sides of its head.
And in one lesson we'd
Have a quick taste
Of what it is like
To go flying in space.
Computerized chairs
That would do what we say.
And desks which fly off
At the end of the day.
In the future we hope
School won't be a pain.
So hurry up future
It's Monday again!!

KELLY GEOGHEGAN   AGE 13   HEIGHINGTON, LINCOLN

children will fly to school with a powered back pack

MAXINE WOOD   AGE 7   PRESTON, HULL

Going to School in the 21st Century

In the morning, if you have overslept, the 'wacky-wacky robot' would lift you up and throw you out of bed. Then the 'washy-washy robot' would pick you up, take you to the bathroom and give you a wash. Then it would put you in the 'dresser-upper machine', which would dress you. Then you would have some wizzy puffs and wizzel berry juice. Time to go to school. Jump into the auto-carrier, press the red button and off to school in thirty seconds. Mr Beep, the robotical teacher, welcomes everyone into class. We turn on our computers. Today is history and we're going to find out what it was like to live in 1992!

2ND PRIZEWINNER – 7s and under

EMMA NIBBS   AGE 7   EAST HAM, LONDON

School in the Next Century

I arrive at school on the dot,
Put my plastic card in the register slot.
It spits it out with determination
And I proceed to my work station.
I switch on my computer in the usual way,
The screen on the monitor says 'Good day'.
It then displays my day's work.
(It does not want me to shirk.)
I work all morning on my computer,
Then fax my efforts to my tutor.
At 12 o'clock I shut down my machine
And make my way to the canteen.
I press a few buttons and turn a wheel
Out comes an additive-free, taste-free meal!

JULIA SHEPHERD   AGE 9   STONY STRATFORD,

MILTON KEYNES

A School Day in the Year 2000

Out of bed, jump in the pool.
Dried and dressed, I'm ready for school.
Put on my coat, check my pocket
Computer's there with my entry docket.

The neighbours come for their morning ride.
The car's charged up, we climb inside.
This solar power is cheap and clean
Stops the coughs, know what I mean?

The docket goes in, my name comes out
Time for lessons, mustn't shout.
My mini computer is raring to go
It needs my input. What do I know?

It's time for lunch, I'm ready to eat.
Tablets first, then the treat.
High nutrition, it's sugar-free
But still tastes good, that's for me.

Out to play, the camera spies.
Much more accurate than the teachers' eyes.
Back to lessons, we're nearly done.
Then time for home to have some fun.

A solar-powered scooter is fun to ride.
Playing with friends, who's turn to hide?
Time to go in to have my tea
One thing hasn't changed and that's *BP*!

CHRISTOPHER PANTLING   AGE 9   POOLE, DORSET

5

THE VOICE OF THE NEXT CENTURY

Sinead McGuinness
Fort William
Belfast
16/2/2050

Dear Stephanie,

I went to the Ulster Folk and Transport Museum in Cuttra, where I bought this paper and pencil in the souvenir shop.

They actually used a bucket and cloth to wash windows, instead of the 'electric window wiper'! In those days they had newspapers instead of news scanners.

There was a quaint thing called a bath with two metal taps stuck into it. They used it instead of a jacuzzi.

In the café they had boiling kettles, not a bit like our push-button boiling points.

In the garden there was a queer thing which looked like two poles with a wire between them. On one of the posts it said 'washing line'. I wonder, did people wash themselves on it?

Have to go now, I'm catching a satellite plane to Australia for a long weekend.

From Sinead.

P.S. You were looking very nice on the phone call you made last Saturday.

1ST PRIZEWINNER – 8s, 9s, 10s

SINEAD McGUINNESS   AGE 8   BELFAST, N. IRELAND

21st Century Pen-pal

21st century pen-pal
you have lots of different things that I
didn't have
when I was your age.
I spoke English.
You speak English and the language of
Europe.
I had the flag of Great Britain.
You have the flag of Europe.
I had money in coins and paper.
You have it in plastic.
I had to make my bed and lots of
other jobs by hand.
You can do these jobs with controls.

But even though you are different
in all these ways are you still the same?
Do you have the sun to warm you?
Do you have people to look after you?
Do you have the rain to water the plants?
I would like to meet you
in the 21st century.

CHLOE JEFFRIES   AGE 6   ELY, CAMBRIDGESHIRE

Dear twenty-first Century

Will there be

and

will our

turn into a

and will

go up and

come

and will

the human population grow or die?

KATHERINE PURSEY   AGE 7   CRANLEIGH, SURREY

A Page From the Diary (2022) of Sophie King-Smith (Age 8)

Yesterday was my great-grandfather's 100th birthday.

In the middle of the day we had a huge family party because we are a huge family. There was my great-grandfather of course, and my great-grandmother, who is going to be 100 later this year, so I expect we'll have another party then, and their three children, and ten grandchildren, and twenty-seven great-grandchildren (including me), and six great-great-grandchildren, and lots of other relations, and a few of my great-grandfather's friends, though most of them are dead. Grampa Dick (that's what we all call him) got a telegram of congratulations from the King. Charles III seems terribly old to me, but of course he's only seventy-three.

Grampa Dick got lots of presents. A lot of them were bottles, mostly bottles of whisky, which Grampa Dick always says is the best thing to drink if you want to live a long time. He looks very old of course and his face is all wrinkled like a walnut, but he's still got quite a lot of white hair left, and he gets around quite quickly on his laser-charged turbo walking frame. His sight is not too bad, but he's pretty deaf. But he remembers everyone's names, right down to the newest great-great-grandchild.

'You're Sophie,' he said to me. 'I wrote some books about you, thirty-odd years ago.'

I said, 'I wasn't born then,' but I don't think he heard.

Grampa Dick has written loads and loads of books for children, mostly stories about animals. Often his books are about pigs, which are his favourites. I shouldn't say this, but actually he does look a bit like a pig now, if you can imagine a wrinkly white-haired pig wearing rather baggy clothes. And he certainly eats like one.

There were all sorts of things to eat at the party, including Grampa Dick's favourites, like smoked salmon with scrambled eggs, and Cumberland sausages (like I said, he loves pigs), and strawberries and cream, and he was shovelling them all in and chomping away and grunting with pleasure.

I saw my great-grandmother dig him in the ribs with her elbow and say something (I expect it was 'You're eating like a pig') but he didn't hear (or pretended not to – I think perhaps he only hears what he wants).

And he had lots to drink too, which must have made him sleepy, I suppose, because at the end of the meal my grandfather proposed my great-grandfather's health, and then everybody clapped and cheered like mad, and then people shouted 'Speech, Grampa Dick! Speech!'

But he was fast asleep in his chair, snoring.

He woke up just as we were all getting ready to be beamed back home. I just happened to be near as they were getting him up on to his feet, and I heard someone say, 'Good job he's got the zimmer to hang on to', and I shouted, 'Many happy returns, Grampa Dick', and he must have heard me because he said, 'I need three more,' and I said, 'Why?' and he said, 'Because *my* great-grandfather lived to be $102\frac{3}{4}$, and I'm going to beat him.'

I wonder if he will?

DICK KING-SMITH

34 Saturn Way
Glexbase 8
M. Station h746
GM8 74H
12 October 2092

Dear Samantha,

I am writing to you via a new invention. It enables us to send letters through time.

What is it like in the 20th century? I have been doing a project on it, at school. It must be really hard work! Imagine having to cook your own food!!

Do you have to write on paper at school? We have a computer each at school, that we carry round to all our lessons. It is quite small, and we just use different micro disks for each lesson (that's a type of computer disk).

We don't have to cook our food. We have an Autocuisine. We just type in the food we want, and it comes out, cooked and ready to eat!! We don't have to go shopping for food, either, we just send our order, via computer, and it gets delivered. You can buy almost anything by computer now, but if you want you can go to the shop to buy things too.

We don't have telephones any more, we can contact people by our computers, or use our phone vision. This is like a telephone, but with a camera attached, so you can see the person you're talking to. For entertainment, we have video, computer or hologram games, there is also a new game just come out, where you sit in a chair, put a headset on and it is like a simulator ride! Don't worry, we still have the classics, like Nintendo, Sega and Virtuality. We also have 3D Holo-tele, where the action is projected into your room as a hologram.

There were lots of wars in the 20th century, weren't there? We haven't had any wars, or aggressions of any kind, for fifty-two years now, which is just as well, as we now have enough weapons to blow up the entire universe!

I had better stop writing now, as there is a limited weight on this Letter-

Through-Time scheme. Please write back, it would be so interesting to hear from you.

Best wishes,
Lisa Black

ABBY JONES   AGE 13   DORRINGTON, SHREWSBURY

21st Century Holiday Centre
London
WC1 2BP
16.8.02

Dear Kate,

I am enjoying my holiday in 2002. We entered the time machine at 10am and arrived here thirty seconds later. Cars are a thing of the past, every car was grinded up in 1996 and turned into fuel! The main means of transport is something called a fly-a-mobile, which is a bit like an aeroplane but is much smaller. It can seat up to ten people, has wheels like a tractor and runs on recycled rubbish.

Blue Peter is different because two of the four presenters are robots! The robots' names are Micro and Chip, the humans' names are Mars and Venus. The Blue Peter pets are two moon moles called Neil and Armstrong.

Schools are run by robots and each child has their own computer. This is a quick way of teaching and school only lasts for three hours. This gives children plenty of time to play with their solar powered skateboards.

It is quite nice in the future but I do miss being able to go outside without wearing an anti-pollution mask.

Must go now as I want to see the green and black sunset.

Love from

Lauren.

P.S. You do achieve your ambition of being an astronaut.

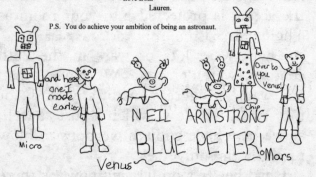

LAUREN WILLIS   AGE 10   HORSHAM, WEST SUSSEX

6

GADGETS GALORE

New Trainers

These new trainers will fly you to school
They fly really fast and they don't need much
    fuel.

They're better than pumps and they're better
    than disk
They fly really smoothly and start really
    brisk.

If you live in Glasgow and you leave at three
You'll make it to London just before tea.

You can buy these new trainers for 100
    pounds flat
I don't know 'bout you but I'll think about
    that!

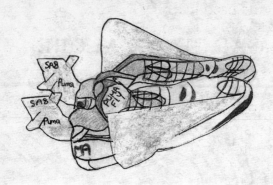

Now you've seen my picture of my new
   trainers flying
I know the next trainer that you will be
   buying.

ROSS INGERBRIGTSEN   AGE 7   KIRKCALDY, FIFE

The Mailalogue June 2000

All Over Protection Spray   Price £5.60

This spray is twenty-four hours protection
from *all* harmful rays. (Ideal for newborn
baby to the elderly). A non-sticky, non-
fragrant oil. And it softens skin and prevents
ageing effects! The syphoned bottle contains
sixty applications and you can refill bottles at
any chemist for just £2.50. The natural

ingredients used include:
camomile, witch hazel
and rose-water. The spray
comes in three different
colours, ultramarine,
navy blue and bright red,
but when sprayed on
merges in to match
the colour of your skin.

Telephone Speech Interpreter   Price £285

A complete communication system for use
with anyone in *any* country. Instantly
converts your words to listener's own
language. With attached microphone to
programme any voice or accent.

Floating Air Bed   Price £110 size 2 m × 1 m

For indoor use only. The inflatable bed floats
approximately one metre above ground level.
Completely cushions your body, adapting to
the user's shape. It is good for muscular pains,
and aiding complete relaxation and
enjoyment. You can choose your own pattern
– just send a sample of the one you want. It
gives out controlled heat. Completely
portable.

SIBELL BARROWCLOUGH   AGE 10   WIVELISCOMBE,

SOMERSET

The Book of the Future

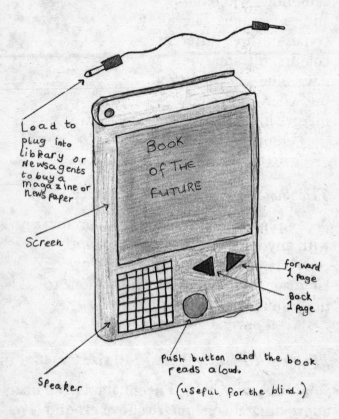

Load to plug into library or Newsagents to buy a magazine or newspaper

Screen

BOOK OF THE FUTURE

forward 1 page

Back 1 page

push button and the book reads aloud.

(useful for the blind.)

Speaker

This is the book of the future. Each person has their own book. It is not made from trees. When you buy a magazine or newspaper, you pay your money and plug the book into a computer, which loads the pictures and words into your book. When you go to the library, you plug your book in and the library computer gives you a new book.

ADAM KING   AGE 6   THETFORD, NORFOLK

Video Phone

In the future, we will have video phones, which will tell the time, have a screen to see who's ringing you and translator so you can understand people from other countries. Communication will change a lot in the future.

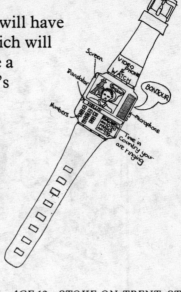

CHRISTOPHER COPE   AGE 12   STOKE-ON-TRENT, STAFFS

When you brush your teeth with this toothbrush little sensors in the head tell you when you have Something wrong with your teeth

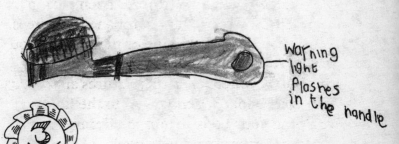

warning light flashes in the handle

3RD PRIZEWINNER – 7s and under

CLAIRE KERRIN   AGE 5   COMBER, CO. DOWN

Morning Work-out

AMY SIMPSON   AGE 13   ULVERSTON, CUMBRIA

New Year's Eve 1999

Nineteen ninety-nine.
Midnight on my mind.
Soon the twentieth century
Will be left behind.

I lived through two world wars.
Got me medals and me scars.
And me flaming poppy.
But no thank you, world war three.

I can't be far from the grave.
After all, I'm only a hundred and five.
But I've got a microwave
And thank God, I'm alive.

It's never been the same,
That quiet country lane
Where we picked blackberries as a child.
Now these motorized skateboards drive me
    wild.

So I sit here all alone
By this rented video-phone,
Waiting for a call from those great-
    grandchildren of mine.
Will any of them remember it's midnight
    nineteen ninety-nine?

Will they give me a beep, a boop or a beam?
You never know with these new-fangled
    machines.

JOHN AGARD

7

READ ALL ABOUT IT!
IT'S THE YEAR 2000

100 Today

LONDON 8th August 2000

REPORTER: Anthony Carroll

Queen Elizabeth, formerly the Queen Mother, today celebrated her 100th birthday amid nationwide jubilations.

The nations favourite royal started the day with a quiet family gathering at Clarence House. Her daughter, Queen Elizabeth the King Mother, who abdicated earlier this year in favour of her son, due to deteriorating health, arrived first with Prince Philip, their car struggling to get through the vast crowds gathered. Next to arrive were King Charles and Queen Diana with their youngest son, Harry (15), on holiday from school at Gordonstoun. Elder brother William (18) arrived soon afterwards, on leave from the Royal Navy, where he is following in the footsteps of his father and uncle.

The Princess Royal arrived with her second husband, her son Peter with his wife, and her daughter Zara with her fiancé.

Prince Andrew drove himself, with daughters Eugene and Beatrice as back-seat passengers. Youngest grandson, Prince Edward, the country's most eligible batchelor, arrived amid great uproar from the female members of the crowd. Much speculation has been around recently regarding his many companions, but today he was decidedly alone.

The usual birthday greetings were sung and Her Majesty defied doctors' orders and walked to greet her people.

Later in the evening a gala party was held in her honour, which many foreign heads of state attended, among them were American President, Jesse Jackson. Prime Minister, Paddy Ashdown, Opposition leader, Robin Cook and Tory leader, Sebastian Coe, were also present. Among the many celebrities were the latest Aussie pop success, Ben Guerens (formerly Toby Mangle in *Neighbours*) and the new darling of the big screen, Emilia Pavarotti (15), daughter of the opera singer. One of the last celebs to arrive was reformed temptress Madonna, with her husband, Jimmy Nail, who, together with their two young children, are currently guests of Prince Edward.

Across the country many street parties were thrown, one of the largest of which was in Teignmouth, Devon, where 5,000 children were treated to fun, games and food along the seaside promenade.

HAPPY BIRTHDAY YOUR MAJESTY

ANTHONY CARROLL   AGE 11   TEIGNMOUTH, DEVON

Atlantic Tunnel Opens – Monday 1 April 2000

At 9.30 a.m. this morning, history was made when the trains took to the tracks for the very first crossing of the Atlantic by underground tunnel. At around 1 p.m. both the UK and the USA trains passed by each other. The super-speed trains, each with 200 cars and carrying 600 people, then sped on to their destinations, arriving safely at 4 p.m.

Following Old Routes

The tunnel, constructed along the same route as the cables laid by the Great Western back in the 20th century, cost over a million billion pounds, but is expected to attract huge profits.

Thrilling Trip

Speaking to passengers arriving here in the UK this evening, the trip sounds thrilling, with videos on board showing the Atlantic above. Several passengers will definitely be repeating the trip, and one lady we spoke to is making the return trip tomorrow.
Ben Francis reporting for *Link Worldwide News*.

BEN FRANCIS   AGE 8   RADLETT, HERTS

This is the 6 O'Clock News From the BBC World Service, Stardate 2058

The first conference of the Galactic Nations is being held on the moon next month, for talks on space pollution and to exchange views on the epidemic of Martian Measles that has steadily increased over the past year.

In Manchester today, the Lord Mayor declared Manchester as the first ozone-friendly city in the UK. All cars were banned, except electric vehicles and man-powered transport, all polluting industries have been closed down.

Although the last surviving pair of elephants died out over twenty years ago, scientists are making efforts to repopulate the species by releasing the first ten artificial elephants created from the cells of the extinct pair.

Scientists have unveiled the first zero-calorie-containing Mars bar. A spokesperson from Choc-a-holics Anonymous said 'Chocolate lovers everywhere don't need to be ashamed of their addiction any more.'

And today we are all wearing gold noses to help raise money for children in need. The money will be used to send deprived children from Britain to Jupiter Disney – free transport is being provided by Virgin Spaceways Ltd.

TANIA PEDLEY   AGE 12   ABERGELE, CLWYD, N. WALES

Environmental Echo

EXCLUSIVE INTERVIEW WITH THE GREEN PARTY, WILL THEY BE THE NEW GOVERNMENT? SEE PAGE 7

October 2000
Volume 3, Number 10

OZONE OUT!

EXCLUSIVE

By JOHANNA WESTWOOD
in Nottingham, England

The only Country still protected by Ozone layer.

OZONE WIPE OUT! - IS HELP ON IT'S WAY?

Yesterday scientists in America revealed news of the ozone layer over Britain. They say it is down to the bare minimum, and if no action is taken quickly, then perhaps there will be no ozone layer left to protect us from the harmful rays of the sun. Also they have revealed that if the ozone isn't saved within the next year or so, then there will be no chance of saving it at all.

The scientists believe that they have found a way to make the ozone reproduce itself, the only problem that they have come across with this solution, as of yet, is that the toxic chemicals we use must be cut down to a very minimum, or be completely abolished, or else the newly repaired ozone will only last for a short while, before it is wiped out completely.

New hope from government!

All countries will be meeting to have a conference, about banning all, or most of the toxic chemicals, and hopefully a treaty will be signed, to prevent anything being made, that could in any way endanger the ozone.

One of the scientists is quoted as saying "I hope that everyone will listen to what is being said about the ozone, and act accordingly. After the success of saving the rain forests, our world is gradually becoming a better place in which to live, and we hope that as with the rain forests, the public will help us fight to save our world."

MOVE TO MARS

The first expedition to Mars is due to take place in 2 weeks today. The group will consist of 3 men, and 3 women, from America, England and Russia.

These people will be filming the planet, and taking samples of the air, the surface and recording the temperature throughout the duration of their stay.

They will spend a year living in their space shuttle, and recording information, to help scientists have a better idea of what life on Mars would be like. Although they already know that the planets surface is too cold for humans to live on at the moment, they believe that if they spray C.F.Cs into the air, then the planet will heat up to a certain temperature, and all ice-caps will melt, and oxygen will be released.
Continued on page 2.

TELEVISION -12-14   LETTERS -16   JOHN MAJOR -4   STARS -5

JOHANNA WESTWOOD   AGE 15   NEWARK, NOTTS

8

ZOOMING TO THE MOON

Travelling into Space

When I travel into space I can see
the 21st century looking at me.
I am going to the moon in a big space rocket.
I take my cuddly teddy and my round polly
   pocket.
The Earth looks like a bouncy ball floating in
the dark. I'm going to see my Granny and she
lives in Lunar Park.
I sometimes go to see my Aunty Beryl on
   planet Mars.
It takes a long time to get there and we have
   to go very far.

JULIA KINSBURY   AGE 7   HENLEY, OXON

Plan Your Family Holiday Trip to the Moon

HANNAH COLEBROOKE AGE 13 WATFORD, HERTS

Letter to Parents

SAINT THOMAS MORE R.C. V.A. MIDDLE SCHOOL

Norwich
Norfolk

3 September 2000

Dear Parents,

For the Year Sevens last trip with Saint Thomas More, we will be taking YR7W to Mars. We will leave on Monday 20 November at 8.30 a.m. and return on Friday 25 at 5.30 p.m. We will travel by the latest 'EXIPIC SHUTTLE' which will pick us up from the Hydra Centre on Bluebell Lane. It has room for two to a seat because, even though it is the fastest vehicle to get us there, it will take us four hours. The cost of this trip will be   150 (Philarunes). This amount, along with the slip below, should be returned by 1 November 2000.

The children may to wear anything they like. Cameras are allowed, but they are not our responsibility (unlike the kids!).

We will be staying at the spacetel 'Star-Space Enterprise' – three to a room. On our way there, we will be passing the Milky Way, Mercury, and Venus. We will not be staying on Mars for the whole trip, we will visit Saturn, Uranus, and possibly Pluto. We have a guide who says with the latest cool suit we might be able to visit the Sun, which will be good fun!

The children will be able to bring up to 50 (Philarunes) for spending money.

More details later.
PLEASE RETURN SLIPS
QUICKLY!

Yours sincerely
Charlotte Dunne
(Headteacher)

Name of child _____

Signed_____

Class_____

Paid (tick box) ☐

CHARLOTTE DUNNE   AGE 11   NORWICH, NORFOLK

People who have space ships travel to other planets

MAKing friends With an atien from another Planet.

JAMIE WALSH   AGE 10   UCKFIELD, EAST SUSSEX

Daniel's Holiday Guide to the Universe

Now listen up, all you readers out there, if you are looking for a holiday, have I got a holiday for you. Yep, you've guessed it, it's a space holiday and I guess it's just the place for you! You travel by a luxurious space bus. When you are in space, you link up with an orbiting gotel (a galactic hotel). There, you

can experience for yourself the pleasure of
having the effect of weightlessness and
secondly, having the world under your feet.
Another attraction is the view, which is
spectacular. Every twelve hours, an
intergalactic taxi takes off from the gotel and
heads off towards the moonbase. You can stay
at the moonbase as part of your holiday, the
length of time depends on you. At the
moonbase, all amenities are open twenty-four
hours of the day. The amenities include a
gym, in which you can do aerial dancing,
formation spinning and slowed down
trampolining. There's a swimming-pool with
a gravity-making machine, four bars and five
restaurants in which the latest gourmet
specialities are prepared by some of the best
cooks in the galaxy. There's also a checkout
where you can change your money into moon
currency.

If you are wondering where you are going
to get your shopping done, wonder no more,
because on the moon, about three miles west
of the moon resort, is a supermarket, which
sells all you could ever need. You may also
want to visit the famous lunar sweet market
where you can sample some of the galaxy's
finest sweets. For adventurous types, there's a
touring line which takes people sight-seeing
around the moon in twenty-four hours.

DANIEL PIERCY   AGE 9   SHEFFIELD

GREETINGS FROM PLUTO

January 2001   POSTCARD

Had a good trip
No hold ups at the
Milky Way These
new snuttle rockets
are very fast. The
weather is O.K. only
one meteorite
shower so far.
The natives are
friendly and the
scenery fabulous

from David

The Presenters
Blue Peter
BBC Television
London
England
Planet Earth

3
PRIZE

3RD PRIZEWINNER – 8s, 9s, 10s

DAVID BROOK   AGE 8   PETERBOROUGH, LINCOLNSHIRE

Competition Winner

Ian was really excited. He had won a competition to go in a spaceship around the moon. The spaceship was called the *Blue Peter*. The *Blue Peter* was about to be launched . . . 5.4.3.2.1 blast off! They soared into space at 100 miles an hour. Ian sat next to John Leslie and listened as he told him about the trip. They saw the hot, hot sun, Venus, Mars and Pluto and all the other planets. They came to the moon. They stopped. Ian went on a short space walk. He jumped high, he called 'whooppee'. Ian picked up some moon dust to take home. They came back down to Earth and Ian was presented with his *Blue Peter* badge.

IAN ROBOTHAM   AGE 7   HARROGATE, YORKS

Holiday to the Moon

We are going on holiday
We are going quite soon
We are not staying on the earth
We are zooming to the moon.

GARETH MAHONEY   AGE 6   SALISBURY, WILTSHIRE

9

SAVE OUR PLANET!

Do You Remember, Mum . . .

Do you remember, Mum, when you used to
peel vegetables – now simply press a button
And bingo you have a potato tablet.

Do you remember, Mum, when you hoovered
the carpet – now the carpet sucks up the dirt
itself.

Do you remember, Mum, when you used
coins – now all you need is your smart card. By
thewaydon'tIstillhavesomecoinsinthatoldbox?

Do you remember, Mum, when you walked
along the pavement – now the pavement
moves instead.

Do you remember, Mum, when we could go for a walk without an oxygen mask . . . That was when the ozone hole was tiny.

Do you think things were better then, Mum, or are they better now??

LUKE LOWRIE   AGE 7   BUCKHURST HILL, ESSEX

CHANGE IT FOR ME

Oh mum tell me please
what was it like for you?
Were there birds and trees and beautiful seas?
pretty clothes better than these
silver suits and boots.
What was a house?
Was it like this a big silver dome?
What were flowers,
did they smell sweet,
better than these smells of heat?
Was the winter cold and refreshing?
Was there snow and big big slopes
which children would ride on
with wooden boards?
Oh mum! why is it like this!
I want your world it must be better than this
I don't like this war and death
Please mum change it for me.
From this acid rain and silver domes
to houses and birds and beautiful seas.
answer me mum can you, can you
CHANGE IT FOR ME.

By Gurvinder Kaur Chadha

GURVINDER KAUR CHADHA   AGE 13

SPARKHILL, BIRMINGHAM

The Customs Officer

'Lifeline Airways announces the departure of flight LL1999. Destination: the 21st century. Will all passengers go through the security gate. Thank you.'

'Have you anything to declare, sir? No? OK, go through. Madam? Yes? Go through the green desk, please. Sir? No? Would you mind if I checked, please? Put your suitcases on here. Now, open them for me, please.'

'What's this? Famine? In Africa too? I don't know how you thought you could hide this! I'm afraid that you cannot possibly take famine through. Now let's look inside the second case.

'Brazilian rain forest? Where did you get this? Rain forest is far too precious to take with you – I didn't even know there was any left. It would only be mistreated on the other side. Next suitcase, please.

'Oh!! How horrible! Tiger skins, fur coats, rhinoceros horns, elephant ivory? This must be stopped. These are definitely not going with you. Put these with the others, please. Open the next one.

'War? I am sorry, sir, but you cannot possibly want to take this – confiscate this now! Last suitcase, please.

'What? This is global warming!! No, sir – I cannot possibly ignore it. This is a very serious issue indeed. Take this away. Global warming definitely cannot go with you – it will destroy the world!!

'Well Mr Earth, I am sorry, but you certainly cannot go through into the 21st century with all of these problems. Come back again when you have solved them. Next please!'

SUZY HARDING   AGE 15   SIDCUP, KENT

Shopping List for 21st Century

A big tin of food for everyone
A packet full of countryside
A box of fresh air
A bottle of hope
A bag of peace
And don't forget lots of fun

CAPELLA REW   AGE 7   TAUNTON, SOMERSET

Homecoming

My name is Max and I'm a Martian.

No, don't get me wrong. I've not got a scaly skin and six eyes. I'm a boy, a human, born here on the red planet fifteen years ago. All my life's been lived under a dome and most of my friends – there's only a few of us here – take this for granted. But my Great-Gran calls it a plastic life. On Earth, she says, the blue sky was the dome and white clouds sailed across it, and in spring – and here she always gets trembly and upset and her chins wobble, for she was too old to have had her face fixed by the Rejuvenation Programme – in spring, she whispers, the leaves and flowers came out and the little birds . . . 'We've got sun and rain!'

'We've got sun and rain!'

'Time-tabled weather!'

'We've got flowers, Great-Gran!'

'Synthetic rubbish! Yuck! Everything regulated! Everything boring!'

I had to agree. Life on Mars is dull.

'People are afraid, that's why. Having to leave Earth after those wars and all that pollution scared 'em witless,' she goes on. 'Not that we had much in the way of wits, or else we wouldn't have wrecked our beautiful planet.'

'We were the lucky ones, Great-Gran. We got away,' I said.

'To be bored stiff,' she sniffed.

'She's right,' sighed my friend Jenny. 'I'd like an adventure.'

We're the only living things on Mars, the ones who escaped from the wrecked Earth, about a hundred of us – great-grandparents, grandparents, parents, children – all living in a compound made up of indestructible, synthetic material, leading a mainly indoor life, since outside is only a desolate, barren landscape. We make our own food and water in the laboratories inside the compound.

'Life sounds as if it was much more exciting on earth than it is here,' went on Jenny.

'How I'd love to go back. It is my dream,' said Great-Gran.

'Let's go,' said Jenny.

And so an idea was born.

There was one person on Mars even older than my Great-Gran, Frederick Morse, the greatest of all the scientists who brought us here long ago. We talked to him.

'Can we go back?' half a dozen of us young ones asked.

Our parents were horrified. They liked the dull security of their semi-underground existence. They felt safe under the dome. But some of the older ones and some of us, opened up the large out-building where the spaceship was. Frederick Morse supervised its over-haul.

'Yes, it can be done. The spaceship will function. If we want to go back to Earth, we can.'

'Yes, yes,' we cried. Great-Gran and Jenny started packing.

But our parents and many grandparents tried

to stop us.

'It's not safe! You mustn't go! The radiation! The pollution! The danger! Stay here!'

My father was so angry, he hit me. No one ever hit anyone in the compound. Jenny was locked in.

'You can't lock me in or stop me,' cried Great-Gran.

She and Frederick called a meeting. It was wild and stormy, but in the end it was agreed that those who wanted to leave, could.

At last, all was ready. Goodbyes were said, tears were shed, and we were on our way, a funny collection of people: Frederick and Great-Gran, six grandparents and ten of us young ones. I sat there, more excited than I'd ever been in all my life.

Months had been spent calculating the best spot to land, the least contaminated area, and what to do when we got there.

'It'll probably be full of yellow monsters,' I said.

'I'll soon deal with them. I'll shoot 'em with a ray gun,' said Great-Gran.

'No time to be bored,' I said.

'But *what* shall we find there?' asked Jenny. 'That's the question.'

'Home,' answered Great-Gran. 'And *this* time we shan't wreck it.'

GENE KEMP

HOVER – TOURS

VISIT U.K. ISLES AT BARGAIN PRICES...

..... JUST $3500

NORTH WEST HIGHLAND ISLES

ISLE OF GRAMPIAN

SOUTH CUMBERLAND ISLAND

PENNINE ISLES

CAMBRIAN ISLAND

UK ISLES

EXPLORE ANCIENT CAVERNS, SCUBA-DIVING AROUND THE OLD CITIES OF EXETER, CARDIFF, DUNDEE, 5 STAR SERVICES.

ISLE OF EXMOOR

RING:
555-33-11-28

The 21st Century Discovery

I found a box
unopened, sealed perfectly.
On it was a label,
it said 'don't open until the 21st century.'
I took it with me right back home,
(it weighed about a tonne.)
I sat there and looked at it,
and filled with great temptation,
I opened the box and took a peep inside.
What I saw first amazed me,
and filled me with delight.
There were the most amazing things.
You name it it was there.
Television was smelly vision,
cars flew in the air,
Robots, doing all our work
were seen everywhere.
I then looked in another place,
what I saw filled me with grief,
The country was a desert,
nothing seemed to live.
There was a building site,
full of fumes and dirt.
Nothing could live with such pollution.
I saw a hunter fire his gun,
and wipe out the last species apart from man.
Only man was left,
and he too would soon be gone.
I took that box and sealed it tight,
and flung it in the ocean,

using all my might.
So much for man and all his technology.
Why can't all creatures,
of this earth live in harmony?

PATRICK WIDDESS   AGE 13   CAMBRIDGE

21st Century Rap

Dear Spirit of the 21st century
I want a nice clean world waiting for me.
I want the whales and the elephants to be free
And all the little animals to be happy.
I don't want the dirt and I don't want the
    noise
And I don't want the very dangerous toys.
I want the toys to be safe and good and fun
And for there to be enough for everyone.
I want the food to be healthy and still taste
    nice.
I want to share it with the children who just
    have rice.
I don't want to forget that we are all friends.
If we don't care for our world it will come to
    an end.
If we try to be friends and stop the war
Then there won't be suffering any more.
If you hear my message it will be just great
But if we don't work together it will be too
    late.

EMMA McDERMOTT   AGE 6   SURBITON, SURREY

The Tree's Life in the Year 2000

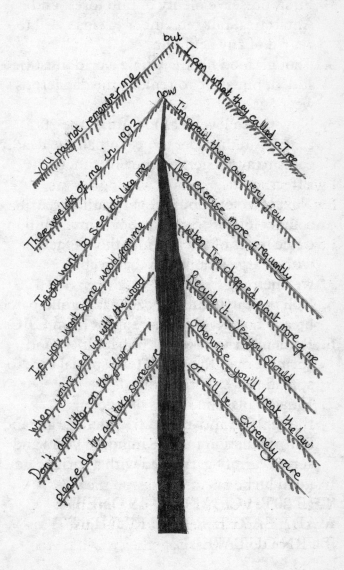

HOLLY MARGETTS   AGE 9   STONE, STAFFS

Recipe for a Perfect 21st Century Earth

1. First, preserve plenty of rain forest and Antarctica, but remember to rinse well to get rid of any acid rain.
2. Enough food for the whole world must be added, but sieve to remove the dangerous weapons.
3. Now take a level teaspoonful of the 20th century, remember to peel off all the deadly gases to avoid getting the Greenhouse Effect.
4. Next take some buildings, graffiti-free of course, lots of animals, about three million cubic miles of sea and mix them together with a large amount of changeable weather.
5. Roll the earth into the ozone layer and patch up any holes which may appear from CFCs.
6. Remember to take lots of happiness and sprinkle over the earth, take special care to spread it evenly though.
7. Finally, place in hands of a good, thoughtful, anti-racist, friendly, caring and fair population for one hundred years and serve warmly garnished with a sprig of good luck.

THE 20TH CENTURY IS ONE WE MADE EARLIER BUT IT DIDN'T TURN OUT WELL.

ERIKA BUZINK   AGE 14   KIDDERMINSTER,
WORCESTERSHIRE

Life in the 21st Century

C is for 21st century in seven years time.
E is for energy we all have to save.
N is for noise-free, that's how cars will have
  to be.
T is for trams, our new mode of transport.
U is for united, peace at last.
R is for recycling, let's save our planet.
Y is for you, we can't do it without you.

STEPHANIE BUDD   AGE 9   BARROW UPON SOW,
LEICESTERSHIRE

10

PROTECT OUR ANIMALS

Now It Is Time to Be Kind

Now it is time to be kind
Put the animals' welfare in your mind.
Don't squash hedgehogs on the road
The motorway is dangerous for toads.

Be kind to whales, there are not many left in
   the sea.
It's up to you and me.
Elephants are wonderful and rare
These creatures need our care.

Let animals be free from cages and pens.
No more cruelty for pigs and hens.
The future is not far away.
Let's keep all the animals we have today.

KIRSTEN 1 . ER   AGE 7   DURHAM

The News 1 October 2000

Nessie is to be a mummy.

The long-necked monster called Nessie came out of the water today and laid seven eggs. The people of Scotland are happy.

SAM HARTREY   AGE 5   CARDIFF, S. WALES

"BUT MUMMY I WANT TO SEE THE REAL PANDAS"

RACHEL GARLICK   AGE 15   LUTON, BEDS

Blue Peter in the Year 2001

'Hello, and welcome to a brand new year of *Blue Peter*. Starting off the year, we shall be launching a new charity to save all the animals on Earth. We sent Johnafolus to make a report on that old forbidding planet.'

'Welcome to this freezing cold planet. I expect you can all feel it through your five sense fact-o-visions. This animal here is called a dog. As you can see it has a long thing hanging off the back, which is called a tail. Now, this species is one of the rarest animals left on this deserted planet, and here is a paw print of an animal that became extinct seven years ago. It is called a Panda Bear. If you want to help the remaining animals, please send any of your old Martian Miascos in a disked addressed envelope to:

>   *Blue Peter* Appeal
>   M.T. Box 9267
>   Zephalon Goddard
>   Mondarsy
>   MN6 LZ641 MARS

'On a piece of paper, put your namus and addressi. In return for your Miascos we shall send you a pack containing posters, stickers and facts about all the Earth animals. Now, back to you, Dianafolus, in the Studiarum.'

'Thank you, Johnafolus. Please, please help us to help the animals of Planet Earth by sending in your old currency.

'If you are a bit peckish, why not watch Jennyfolus prepare a snack that will make your mouth water just by smelling it through your five sense f-o-v?'

CAROLINE JENKINSON AGE 11 YARWELL,
PETERBOROUGH

The Daily Globe

RETURNED FROM EXTINCTION!

Today, John Waterman, an intrepid explorer form the African Rainforest, was on his electric elephant, when suddenly a wierd and wonderful animal ran out in front of him. He quickly grabbed his camera and took several snaps of the animal before it uttered a kind of 'Tarzan' call and ran back into the undergrowth. He rushed back to his processing laboratory and developed the photographs. Never having seen such a beast, he went to the library and got a book on 20th Century animals.

He scanned the pages and eventually found what he was looking for. The animal was a gorilla! This animal had not been seen for the past 20 years and was thought to have been extinct.

We asked John Waterman what he felt like after such an experience. He said, " I feel very proud to be the only one who has seen this creature in 20 years." The World Wildlife Fund for Extinct Animals has organised a massive search of the area to see how many of these 'hairy' creatures are really left. The results will be issued in 2 weeks.

JANINE WOODWARD AGE 12 COLEFORD, GLOS

Looking into the 21st Century

Acres of grassland where
    animals roam free
A common sight for all to
    see
Numbers are plenty each
    species can thrive
No longer battling to
    survive
Living as nature intended without the fear
Of the sound of the guns as
    the hunter grows near

Rolling waters displaying
    their colours true
Of emerald green and
    sparkling blue
The underwater kingdom
    can flourish again
Gone is the threat of acid
    rain

Forests adorned by leaves
    unfurled
This truly is a living world
Both plants and animals
    flourishing with ease
Having been protected –
    LONG LIVE THE TREES

Surely the most heart-
    warming sight to see

Is every man, woman and
   child from each country
Living together and joined
   as one
In making our world a place
   full of fun
Where poverty, starvation
   and suffering is rare
Filled only with love and
   people who care

We all have our dreams of an ideal world

ZOE TEBBUTT   AGE 13   MARKET HARBOROUGH,

LEICESTERSHIRE

BRIE CLAIRE DEVINE   AGE 6   LANARKSHIRE, SCOTLAND

Endangered Animals Wordsearch

A	Z	V	P	N	J	M	O	K	N	T	R	A	E	B
F	I	S	H	S	B	O	S	Z	T	S	E	A	U	I
R	A	N	E	O	L	U	P	E	O	A	J	G	N	R
I	S	A	N	R	U	N	E	L	A	N	P	L	I	D
C	G	K	U	E	E	T	T	A	N	L	E	I	A	S
A	J	I	S	C	S	A	E	H	T	H	E	P	R	A
N	P	U	A	O	E	I	R	W	N	A	P	E	Z	D
E	E	L	L	N	A	N	I	E	A	G	G	L	E	N
L	W	H	E	I	T	G	C	U	T	I	W	L	R	A
E	O	N	E	H	U	O	E	L	T	O	R	R	A	P
P	R	G	L	R	R	R	T	B	O	E	K	I	C	T
H	L	I	A	V	T	I	Q	T	A	K	R	A	S	N
A	D	B	E	E	L	L	X	U	E	A	R	K	P	A
N	I	S	L	I	E	L	I	O	N	R	B	C	D	I
T	D	R	O	W	L	A	U	R	A	D	T	A	O	G

AFRICAN
  ELEPHANT
GIANT PANDA
BLUE WHALE
GIANT OTTER
MOUNTAIN
  GORILLA
OKAPI

PARROT
RHINOCEROS
SEAL
SEA TURTLE
TAPIR
TIGER

LAURA AISTHORPE   AGE 8   SHEFFIELD

11

OUT AND ABOUT

Shopping 2000

Shopping in the 21st century will be really easy. Shoppers will arrive at the shop and sit down with a cup of tea. A conveyor-belt will take them around the store. Each shopper will have a card with a code on, which they slot into a computer at each item they wish to buy. The computer saves this in its memory, so when the customers get to the till their shopping is ready packed and added up. They pay with their card and the shopping is delivered in a shuttle car. No money, no trolley to push, and no heavy bags to carry!

JADE CORCORAN   AGE 6   STOKE-ON-TRENT, STAFFS

Four-Decker Bus for the 21st Century

VICKI WALKER   AGE 6   DUNFERMLINE, FIFE

The Superzoom!

Calling all Grannies, Grandpas and O.A.Ps!
The wheelchair is a thing of the past. Old, rusty, slow and a nuisance! That is one way of describing a wheelchair. But entering into the 21st century is a new incredible invention, stand back and make way for the new *Superzoom!*

This new fold-up wheelchair is specially designed for bored Grannies living with their families. Grannies will be delighted with the new *Superzoom!* Not only is it more comfortable and easier to move around in but it also features many hidden extras.

For example, the fifteen gears it proudly posseses means moving around is a lot less difficult especially as *Superzoom* has a steering lever and a small environmentally friendly, solar powered motor.

The chair has a small fitted colour television which enables you to watch knitting and gardening programmes without being moaned at by the Grandchildren who want to watch 'Neighbours'-the soap which is still running even in the 21st century! While you are watching the knitting demonstration on the T.V you can join in by using the knitting machine at the side of the chair which helps with the knitting.

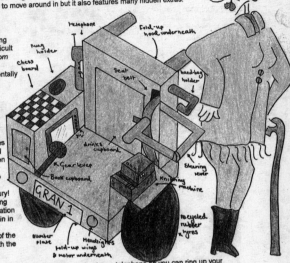

Not only does the chair have a television but it also has a telephone so you can ring up your friends and invite them round for a cup of tea and a gossip about the new people in Number 23 - things still haven't changed since the 20th century!

The most exlusive part of the chair, however, is the set of wings it has which means the chair is able to fly, only at a low altitude but high enough to reach the space bus station where the air bus will take you up to the space hotel you are booked in at!

The fantastic *Superzoom* costs only 74090 ECUs, you can still purchase it using pounds if the shop you buy it at accepts pounds instead of the new 21st century ECUs.

The *Superzoom* chair can be bought at any major superstore or can be purchased by filling in the form below. The delivery is free of charge.

Complete this form and return it to:
'21st Century Gadgets', Mill lane, London, DD3 7GT.
I enclose a cheque for 74090 ECUs.
Name...
Address...
.................Postcode.....................

3RD PRIZEWINNER – 11s to 15s

HARRIET CARMICHAEL   AGE 13   BROUGHTON,

HAMPSHIRE

Rubbish Collection in the 21st Century

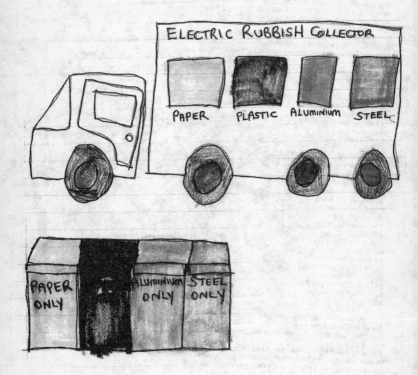

In the 21st century I think rubbish from all the houses will have to be sorted into different coloured dustbins. The rubbish-collectors will then empty them into an electric lorry that has different compartments for all the rubbish to be recycled.

DEBORAH HOUGHTON-LE-CHAPPLE   AGE 7   HILLINGDON,

MIDDLESEX

MacMartians

EATS

Saturn Burger with onion rings	1.00 FC
Moon Burger with Green Cheese	1.10 FC
Venus Vegeburger	1.00 FC
Venusian vegetables in bread crumbs	1.10 FC
Neptune Nuggets – seafood	1.00 FC
Plutos – Hot Dogs	.90 FC
Sun Rays – Solar Cooked Fries	.70 FC

DRINKS

Milky Way Shakes	.60 FC
Black Hole Cola	.50 FC
Jupiter Jaffa Juice	.55 FC

We accept Federation Credits, Alien Access and Alpha Centauri Express.

FINE FOOD AT THE SPEED OF LIGHT!!

TAMISE TOTTERDELL   AGE 9   HUNTLY, ABERDEENSHIRE

HOVERBALL

IT'S FAST, IT'S FRANTIC, IT'S A CROSS BETWEEN SKATEBOARDING AND BASKETBALL AND IT'S PLAYED 5m ABOVE THE GROUND!

HOVERBALL IS PLAYED BY 2 TEAMS OF 6 PLAYERS, EACH TRYING TO GET THE SMALL BALL INTO THE 1m CIRCULAR GOALS, EACH PLAYER HAS A MAGNETIC HOVER BOARD WHICH IS REPELLED BY THE MAGNETIC FLOOR SO IT HOVERS IN THE AIR. THE PADDED FLOOR PREVENTS INJURY TO PLAYERS WHO FALL OFF THEIR BOARDS.

GAMES ARE HIGLY COMPETITIVE, EXTREMELY PHYSICAL AND PLAYED AT DEATH DEFYING SPEEDS, THIS MAKES HOVER BALL THE MOST EXCITING SPORT OF THE 21st CENTURY.

ONE WAY GLASS

PROTECTIVE HELMET

SHOULDER & CHEST PROTECTION

SUPER GRIP GLOVES

BOOTS WITH SLIGHTLY MAGNETIC SOLES

MAGNETIC BOARD

ELLIOTT QUINCE   AGE 15   LUTON, BEDS

The Eco-car

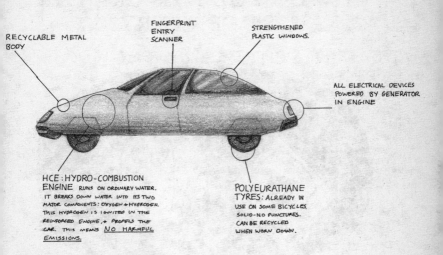

RECYCLABLE METAL BODY

FINGERPRINT ENTRY SCANNER

STRENGTHENED PLASTIC WINDOWS.

ALL ELECTRICAL DEVICES POWERED BY GENERATOR IN ENGINE

HCE: HYDRO-COMBUSTION ENGINE RUNS ON ORDINARY WATER. IT BREAKS DOWN WATER INTO ITS TWO MAJOR COMPONENTS: OXYGEN + HYDROGEN. THIS HYDROGEN IS IGNITED IN THE REINFORCED ENGINE, + PROPELS THE CAR. THIS MEANS NO HARMFUL EMISSIONS.

POLYEURATHANE TYRES: ALREADY IN USE ON SOME BICYCLES SOLID-NO PUNCTURES. CAN BE RECYCLED WHEN WORN DOWN.

ANTHONY BUTCHER   AGE 15   MARLESFORD, SUFFOLK

You might have cars that drive by themselves, then you would have maps in a computer to tell the car where the corners are.

RACHEL BROOKES   AGE 5   MAIDENHEAD, BERKSHIRE

12

HOW DO *YOU* PICTURE THE 21ST CENTURY?

A Future of Hope

The school bell rings and everybody stands up and starts packing away their stuff. Shutting the lid of my personal computer, I stuff it into my bag and proceed towards the door.

'Venus!' a voice calls and seven of us turn to face the teacher, 'You'. He points at me and smiles, 'Are you going to be at Esperanto lessons tonight?'

'Yeah, I should be there,' I tell him, secretly wishing that I didn't have to go, but it is the law to learn the new European language so I have to. I leave the room.

Outside my car is waiting. It is great, ever since the invention of the Space Roller car, the driving age has been reduced to thirteen. For my fourteenth birthday I was given one. It is small and only holds two people. It is red and has a clear bubble roof with a sun-flap. They are so much more convenient, the number of parking spaces has doubled since they were introduced.

Climbing into the driver's seat, I bend my head and stare at the red strip beside the steering wheel. The radio switches on and the music of an oldies group from the early nineties fills the car. A wave of my hand changes the channel and my favourite group, The New Moon Cadets, are thumping out the catchy rhythm of their latest chart-topper.

While riding along in my car, I stare out of the window at the beautiful world passing me by. Environmental issues are a part of everyday life for us in the twenty-first century. We have environmental classes at school and many of our laws are aimed at protecting our planet. All the damage done by past generations is finally repairing itself and we intend to keep our world intact and to make it as perfect as we can, for our children's children, and many future generations to come.

Eventually I pull up outside my house. It is hexagon-shaped and instead of having tiles like the old houses, it has solar panels to work

our TV and other household appliances.
When inside, I mount the escalator up to my
room. My room is Space Silver and very
sophisticated. Pulling off my school uniform
of gold hot-pants edged with feathers, fake of
course, and silver quilted jacket, I put on my
casual outfit of flared trousers with gold and
silver quilted diamonds and grey shirt with
sequins. Dad says he can vaguely remember
flares when he was a child in the seventies.
It's funny how fashion from the past can make
itself so popular many years on, even in a
different century. I turn on my television,
which takes up one whole wall of my
bedroom. Sitting down for a couple of
minutes, I watch a news update on the
construction of the New Moon Motel that Dad
has already booked us into for when it opens.

Pulling out my computer, I flip up the lid
and press the button for the homework file. A
sentence flashes up on the screen. 'WHAT
NEW INVENTIONS HAVE BEEN
INTRODUCED IN THE TWENTY-
FIRST CENTURY AND HOW DO
THEY AFFECT YOUR LIFE TODAY?'

Looking around me, I sit down at my desk
and begin typing. 'The twenty-first century
has brought a whole new meaning to modern
living and . . .' I type and type until there is
nothing else to write.

The twenty-first century means a better life
for everyone. Who knows for sure, but we can

hope and pray that this statement is true, and
that famine, war and many other problems
that hound us constantly now, will fade into
the background like a bad dream.

JENNIFER BIRNIE   AGE 15   INVERNESS, SCOTLAND

My daddy lives in outer space
and my grandad lives on Pluto.
My friend lives on the moon
and I would live there too.

DAVID KINGSBURY   AGE 5   HENLEY, OXON

Intergalactic Estate Agents

£250,000
Four-bedroom detached house
With NEW anti-gravity bricks,
beautiful location on the moon,
with free craters!
South-facing garden,
super view of the Earth
and the stars.
Intergalactic space-bus service every Monday
Special features:
Sky TV, non-gravity carpets
Space furniture and lights.
PHONE: 9090 7124 896

EMMA SOAR   AGE 11   WARE, HERTS

2ND PRIZEWINNER – 11s to 15s

JONATHON TWEMLOW   AGE 14   STAFFORD

The *Radio Times* Monday 6 January 2000

BLUE PETER RETURNS

Tomorrow will see the beginning of the newly modernized series of *Blue Peter*. With a new set, three new presenters and *BP* pet, the new *Blue Peter* series is forecast to be the best yet. With *Blue Peter*'s former presenters John, Diane and Anthea all emigrating to their timeshare log cabin in Alaska, Lewis Bronze was left with the task of finding three new presenters. Their names have not yet been announced, but one of them is said to be small, yellow and noisy with bright-green hair.

The new set will contain three main areas – an interviewing area, 'making' area and stage. There are new couches with in-built microphones, and a video wall, which will help with live link-ups with the rest of the world and beyond. An indestructible, self-cleaning kitchen will be another of the up-to-the-minute features. The huge stage will be where choirs, orchestras, musicians, dancers and actors will perform in the weeks to come.

In the pets corner will be the home of the only living giant panda in the world. She will be replacing Kari and Oki the *BP* cats after their decision to follow their singing career to Japan. There are also several reports planned about the recent extinction of many animals, including the black rhino.

The new series looks as if it will live up to its expectations as the best children's programme in the world, and although life here in the year 2000 has changed in many ways since life in 1992, it must be said that if life goes on, so will *Blue Peter*.

ZARINA SYED   AGE 13   MILL HILL, LONDON

Are You Receiving Me?

MW to BRAIN: Brain! Brain! Come in, please, Brain! Are you receiving me?

BRAIN to MW: This is a recorded message. Hi! This isn't Brain. I am not in. Please leave your message after the pips. Please speak clearly. *Peep! Peep! Peep!*

MW to BRAIN: Come off it! I know you're there.

BRAIN to MW: I am still hanging around inside Head, if that's what you mean, but I'm on holiday. While I'm on the subject of holidays, may I remind you that we are supposed to be walking the dog?

MW to BRAIN: But this is an emergency! Readathon want us to write something about the 21st century.

BRAIN to MW: Why us?

MW to BRAIN: Well, we're supposed to be a writer. We're supposed to have something to say about the 21st century.

BRAIN to MW: But we haven't! We *know* we haven't. We're a pretty dumb writer after all. Never could manage science fiction. Bears and ducks and footballers, that's about our lot. And *please* pay attention to where we are going, you almost walked us into that lamp-post.

MW to BRAIN: Thanks a bundle! Couldn't you give us something serious to say? Like The-

World-Will-Come-To-An-End if we don't do something? A 'Moral Message' to change the world?

BRAIN to MW: Nope!

MW to BRAIN: Why not?

BRAIN to MW: We aren't clever enough. And we've no bright ideas about what the 21st century will be like.

MW to BRAIN: How about a poem? Or a drawing?

BRAIN to MW: Not a poet! Can't draw! And if you don't look where we are going, we'll never make it to the park.

MW to BRAIN: But what *can* we do? The Readathon letter asked us to do it because we are a famous person with ideas, and the letter says they need it now, for the Readathon book and . . .

BRAIN to MW: Tell them we didn't get the letter!

MW to BRAIN: That's pathetic, Brain!

BRAIN to MW: I'm *our* Brain, after all. What did you expect? It might be safer if you let the dog manage the road.

You almost had us under that lorry.

MW to BRAIN: A story, Brain. That's what we expect. There's going to be a whole book full of stories and poems and stuff, and we have got to be in it.

BRAIN to MW: Why us?

MW to BRAIN: Because we're a writer. If we don't write stories for the 21st century then there aren't going to be any! I can't imagine a future world without stories.

BRAIN to MW: There'll always be stories, even in the 21st century, but *we* aren't going to write them.

MW to BRAIN: If *we* don't write the stories for the 21st century, who is going to do it?

MW to BRAIN: Who.

BRAIN to MW: The children who are children now. Some of them are writing already for the Readathon book. It won't be us. It will be them, because the new century will be theirs, not ours. They'll write their

own stories, for their own
time.

MW to BRAIN: You mean . . . hello
twenty-first century,
goodbye us?

BRAIN to MW: Yes. But do pay attention.
We are in the park. Let the
dog off the lead . . . that is
why we came out in the
first place, isn't it? So the
dog could get a run?

MW to BRAIN: Hold on a minute! If these
kids are going to grow up
and write their own stories
for their own century, what
will we do?

BRAIN to MW: We'll read their stories, if
we can understand them.
We might even have time
to relax without all this
think-think-think to bother
_____ _____ _____ walk.

MW to BRAIN: Y-e-s. Yes!

BRAIN to MW: Starting now. This is
Brain, switching off! Over
and out!

MW (much   R-O-V-E-R!
relieved):   R-O-V-E-R!!

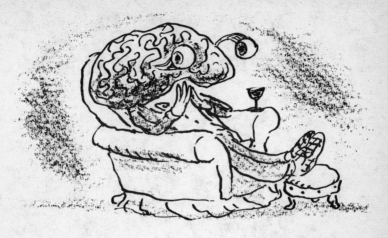

MARTIN WADDELL

13

ANSWERS TO PUZZLES

Futuristic Wordsearch

T	A	R	O	B	E	E	S	C	I	E	N	C	E	S
U	E	O	B	U	Z	M	X	O	Y	P	Z	C	N	D
A	T	C	N	R	E	D	O	M	H	G	Y	E	I	I
N	D	K	H	A	L	J	F	P	V	W	L	J	H	M
O	U	E	O	N	U	Y	S	U	F	L	A	X	C	O
R	R	T	L	R	O	B	O	T	T	D	S	N	A	O
T	A	F	O	C	Q	L	T	E	Q	U	E	B	M	N
S	X	H	G	I	T	G	O	R	K	W	R	P	L	V
A	W	N	R	F	K	C	R	G	N	I	C	E	H	Z
E	S	P	A	C	E	C	I	T	Y	V	F	R	M	M
G	C	G	M	L	L	A	B	C	I	N	O	S	K	A
O	Q	S	D	B	P	R	A	C	E	C	A	P	S	J

Plan Your Holiday Trip to the Moon

Endangered Animals Wordsearch

About Readathon

READATHON is a national reading event which encourages children to read by raising money for sick children. It works just like a sponsored walk or swim, except that the children taking part read books. It encourages children to read recreationally and at the same time fosters their natural desire to help others.

The money raised by READATHON goes to The Malcolm Sargent Cancer Fund for Children and The Roald Dahl Foundation, where it will be spent on providing practical help to children in Britain with cancer, Hodgkin's Disease, leukaemia or other serious blood disorders.

Now in its ninth year, READATHON has already raised five million pounds for charity, and is a regular autumn term event in thousands of schools throughout Great Britain.